AF326634

Antony &
Cleopatra

FOR KIDS
(The melodramatic version!)

For 8-22+ actors, or kids of all ages who want to have fun!
Creatively modified by
Brendan P. Kelso
Cover stage illustrated by Shana Hallmeyer
Cover Characters by Ron Leishman

3 Melodramatic Modifications of Shakespeare's Play
for 3 different group sizes:

8-12 Actors

12-17 Actors

15-22+ Actors

Table Of Contents

Dedicated to Roy R.

One of the best posers I've ever met!

-BPK

For performance rights please see page 6 of this book or contact:

contact@PlayingWithPlays.com

Foreword

When I was in high school there was something about Shakespeare that appealed to me. Not that I understood it mind you, but there were clear scenes and images that always stood out in my mind. Romeo & Juliet, "Romeo, Romeo; wherefore art thou Romeo?"; Julius Caesar, "Et tu Brute"; Macbeth, "Double, Double, toil and trouble"; Hamlet, "to be or not to be"; A Midsummer Night's Dream, all I remember about this was a wickedly cool fairy and something about a guy turning into a donkey that I thought was pretty funny. It was not until I started analyzing Shakespeare's plays as an actor that I realized one very important thing, I still didn't understand them. Seriously though, it's tough enough for adults, let alone kids. Then it hit me, why don't I make a version that kids could perform, but make it easy for them to understand with a splash of Shakespeare lingo mixed in? And voila! A melodramatic masterpiece was created! They are intended to be melodramatically fun!

THE PLAYS: There are 3 plays within this book, for three different group sizes. The reason: to allow educators or parents to get the story across to their children regardless of the size of their group. As you read through the plays, there are several lines that are highlighted. These are actual lines from the original book. I am a little more particular about the kids saying these lines verbatim. But the rest, well... have fun!

The entire purpose of this book is to instill the love of a classic story, as well as drama, into the kids. And when you have children who have a passion for something, they will start to teach themselves, with or without school.

These plays are intended for pure fun. Please DO NOT have the kids learn these lines verbatim, that would be a complete waste of creativity. But do have them basically know their lines and improvise wherever they want as long as it pertains to telling the story. Because that is the goal of an actor: to tell the story. In A Midsummer Night's Dream, I once had a student playing Quince question me about one of her lines, "but in the actual story, didn't the Mechanicals state that 'they would hang us'?" I thought for a second and realized that she had read the story with her mom, and she was right. So I let her add the line she wanted and it added that much more fun, it made the play theirs. I have had kids throw water on the audience, run around the audience, sit in the audience, lose their pumpkin pants (size 30 around a size 15 doesn't work very well, but makes for some great humor!) and most importantly, die all over the stage. The kids love it.

One last note: if you want some educational resources, loved our plays, want to tell the world how much your kids loved performing Shakespeare, want to insult someone with our Shakespeare Insult Generator, or are just a fan of Shakespeare, then hop on our website and have fun:

PlayingWithPlays.com

With these notes, I'll see you on the stage, have fun, and break a leg!

SCHOOL, AFTERSCHOOL, and SUMMER classes

I've been teaching these plays as afterschool and summer programs for quite some time. Many people have asked what the program is, therefore, I have put together a basic formula so any teacher or parent can follow and have melodramatic success! As well, many teachers use my books in a variety of ways. You can view the formula and many more resources on my website at: PlayingWithPlays.com

- Brendan

OTHER PLAYS AND FULL LENGTH SCRIPTS

We have over 25 different titles, as well as a full-length play in 4-acts for theatre groups: Shakespeare's Hilarious Tragedies. You can see all of our other titles on our website here: PlayingWithPlays.com/books

As well, you can see a sneak peek at some of those titles at the back of this book.

And, if you ever have any questions, please don't hesitate to ask at: Contact@PlayingWithPlays.com

ROYALTIES

If you have any questions about royalties or performance licenses, here are the basic guidelines:

1) Please contact us! We always LOVE to hear about a school or group performing our books! We would also love to share photos and brag about your program as well! (with your permission, of course)

2) If you are a group and DO NOT charge your kids to be in this production, contact us about discounted copyright fees (one way or another, we will make this work for you!) You are NOT required to buy a book per kid (but, we will still send you some really cool Shakespeare tattoos for your kids!)

3) If you are a group and DO charge your kids to be in the production, (i.e. afterschool program, summer camp) we ask that you purchase a book per kid. Contact us as we will give you a bulk discount (10 books or more) and send some really cool press on Shakespeare tattoos!

4) If you are a group and DO NOT charge the audience to see the plays, please see our website FAQs to see if you are eligible to waive the performance royalties (most performances are eligible).

5) If you are a group and DO charge the audience to see the performance, please see our website FAQs for performance licensing fees (this includes performances for donations and competitions).

Any other questions or comments, please see our website or email us at:

contact@PlayingWithPlays.com

The 15-Minute or so
Antony & Cleopatra
By William Shakespeare
Creatively modified by
Brendan P. Kelso
8 - 12 Actors

CAST OF CHARACTERS:

TEAM ANTONY & CLEOPATRA:

ANTONY: one of the Roman triumvirate and in love with Cleopatra

CLEOPATRA: in love with Antony and ruler of Egypt

[3]**CHARMIAN:** attendant to Cleopatra

[1]**ENOBARBUS:** mostly faithful supporter of Antony

[4]**EROS:** one of Antony's dudes

[4]**CANIDIUS:** general in Antony's military

TEAM CAESAR:

OCTAVIUS CAESAR: Julius' nephew and a member of the triumvirate

[2]**LEPIDUS:** The third triumvirate (he's not around long)

[3]**OCTAVIA:** Caesar's sister

[2]**AGRIPPA:** one of Caesar's officers

OTHERS:

POMPEY: bad guy who wants to cause trouble [1]

MESSENGER: a messenger, duh

The same actors can play the following part:

[1]ENOBARBUS and POMPEY
[2]LEPIDUS and AGRIPPA
[3]OCTAVIA and CHARMIAN
[4]EROS and CANIDIUS
EXTRAS can be soldiers throughout play

ACT 1 SCENE 1

Cleopatra's palace, Egypt

(enter EROS and ENOBARBUS wearing Egyptian souvenirs)

EROS: Those pyramids were awesome!

ENOBARBUS: Totally! Hey, did you read the National Egyptian this morning?

EROS: Yes! It said Antony, a ruler of Rome, has totally fallen in love with the Egyptian queen, Cleopatra! Speaking of... here's the strumpet's fool now!

(enter ANTONY and CLEOPATRA)

CLEOPATRA: If it be love indeed, tell me how much.

ANTONY: More than the entire Roman empire!

ENOBARBUS: *(aside)* That's a lot!!!

(enter MESSENGER)

MESSENGER: News, my good lord, from Rome.

ANTONY: *(referencing CLEOPATRA)* Can't you see I'm busy?

CLEOPATRA: *(loving the adoration)* Darling, you really should get back to defending Rome.

ANTONY: Let Rome melt! My duty is you, my love.

CLEOPATRA: You're such a kidder. *(grabs his hand)* Let's go check out the Sphinx!

(ANTONY and CLEOPATRA exit)

EROS: *(their mouths agape)* Did you hear what he said about Rome?

ENOBARBUS: Such disrespect!

(ALL exit)

ACT 1 SCENE 2

(enter CHARMIAN and CLEOPATRA)

CLEOPATRA: Charmian, men are weird. First, he wants nothing to do with Rome, and now it's "Rome, Rome, Rome"!!! Hmph!!!

(CHARMIAN nods emphatically saying snide comments)

CHARMIAN: Madam, here comes Antony.

CLEOPATRA: Well that's my cue to exit, bye-bye!

(CLEOPATRA and CHARMIAN exit; ANTONY and MESSENGER enter opposite)

MESSENGER: Sir, your brother lost his battle against Octavius Caesar.

ANTONY: Well, that's a bummer.

MESSENGER: Sir, you do realize if you would've been there...

(ANTONY glares at him)

ANTONY: Excuse me? Taunt my faults?

MESSENGER: What?! I didn't say anything... must have been him! *(points at audience member; ANTONY double claps – SOLDIERS run on and remove MESSENGER)*

ANTONY: Arghhh! I must be gone to Rome. My people need me! *(turns to leave)*

(CLEOPATRA and CHARMIAN enter)

CLEOPATRA: Oh, Antony.

ANTONY: Yes, my dear?

CLEOPATRA: I'm worried when you leave you will not care for me anymore.

ANTONY: Now, my dearest queen, Rome's really messed up, and they need me, The Great Antony! *(strikes a pose)*

CLEOPATRA: But Rome is so far from Egypt.

ANTONY: My precious queen, distance doesn't matter, because my heart is here. Adieu!

(ALL exit)

ACT 1 SCENE 3

Rome

(enter CAESAR and LEPIDUS)

CAESAR: Lepidus, you, Antony, and I rule Rome. The Triumvirate. Yet he continues to leave. As you can tell I am peeved.

LEPIDUS: Caesar, Antony does like to vacation. A lot. But, he's done a lot of great things, 'tis pity him.

CAESAR: No! Pompey thrives in our idleness and we need Antony here, not in Egypt.

LEPIDUS: Agreed, but he's not here.

CAESAR: Antony is one of the best soldiers ever.

LEPIDUS: Again, yes, but not here.

CAESAR: Antony was always nice to my cat.

LEPIDUS: Ugh, Yes, BUT HE'S NOT HERE! Let's get an army together to fight Pompey.

CAESAR: Fine. Let's go!

(ALL exit)

ACT 1 SCENE 4

Cleopatra's palace

(enter CLEOPATRA and CHARMIAN)

CHARMIAN: I have a gift from Antony. *(presents gift to CLEOPATRA)*

CLEOPATRA: Awww... How pretty! Oh, how I miss Antony!

CHARMIAN: He kiss'd this orient pearl. His way of saying... bye-bye with love.

CHARMIAN: Awwww.

CLEOPATRA: I know. *(melodramatically)* I will write him a love letter. EVERY. SINGLE. DAY!

CHARMIAN: A bit smothering, don't ya think?

CLEOPATRA: No. That's loooove! How about this one... O happy horse, to bear the weight of Antony! *(melodramatically)* Eternity was in our lips and in our eyes.

CHARMIAN: Wow, totally gross. Come on, you lovesick fool!

(ALL exit)

ACT 2 SCENE 1

Pompey's house, Italy

(enter POMPEY who addresses audience)

POMPEY: I am about to go into battle against the triumvirate. I hear what you're thinking, 'three against one', BUT! I control the sea, and Mark Antony, their greatest leader, in Egypt sits at dinner. Victory shall be mine!

(enter MESSENGER who hands note)

MESSENGER: A message, sir.

POMPEY: What's this? *(reads)* Caesar and Lepidus have recruited an army against me?! Well, that's a problem!

MESSENGER: Sir, another message... Antony is in Rome, expected.

POMPEY: Well, double poop! My nefarious plans are dwindling with each line of this play! Time to think of another dastardly plan! Soldier, let's go!

MESSENGER: Umm, sir? I'm a messenger.

POMPEY: Look, my odds are diminishing quickly, you're a soldier now. *(shoves sword into MESSENGER'S hands)* Now, let's go SOLDIER!

MESSENGER: Yes, sir!

(ALL exit, marching)

ACT 2 SCENE 2

House of Lepidus, Rome

(enter ANTONY and LEPIDUS from one side; CAESAR from other)

LEPIDUS: Please use soft and gentle speech with Caesar.

ANTONY: I shall use as hard and honest words as I feel.

(CAESAR and ANTONY meet at center, ANTONY strikes a pose)

CAESAR: Sit.

ANTONY: No. You sit, sir.

CAESAR: Nay, then. I should say myself offended. Your being in Egypt, while we need your military support. Specifically, me!

ANTONY: Caesar, look at you, you're very talented and don't need me!

CAESAR: *(unsuccessfully trying to pose like ANTONY)* I KNOW THAT! But... that doesn't matter! You should be here, not gallivanting around Egypt!

LEPIDUS: Men! Stop bickering. Time calls upon's: Of us must Pompey presently be sought.

ANTONY & CAESAR: Huh?

LEPIDUS: You know... our looming battle. *(they reluctantly nod in agreement)* An idea... Antony, why don't you date Caesar's sister? Then it's all in the family, and you will prove your allegiance.

CAESAR: Yeah? What do you say... Brother?

ANTONY: Date her? *(aside)* It's a smart political move. BUT, Cleopatra will NOT be happy. BUT, I should stay faithful to Rome. BUT, I'm sure Cleopatra would totally understand, right? I mean, what could possibly go wrong? *(to CAESAR)* Let's do it!

(they shake hands)

CAESAR: Great! Now let's go take on Pompey!

ANTONY: One for all!

CAESAR and LEPIDUS: And all for one!

(ALL exit)

ACT 2 SCENE 3

Cleopatra's palace

(enter CLEOPATRA and MESSENGER, opposite)

MESSENGER: Madam, a message about Antony.

CLEOPATRA: *(melodramatically overreacting)* What?! Oh no!!! Antonius dead!!!

MESSENGER: No, no. He's well, but yet…

CLEOPATRA: I do not like, 'but yet'. But yet could mean a lot of things! But yet he is dead! *(ugly cries)*

MESSENGER: Madam, he is well… just… dating someone.

CLEOPATRA: WHAT?! Ohhh… he's going to wish he were dead!!!

MESSENGER: Okayyyy, on that note, I'm outta here! *(exits frantically)*

CLEOPATRA: No wait! *(MESSENGER returns, scared)*

MESSENGER: Y-Y-Yes.

CLEOPATRA: Go back and spy on her. Tell me what she looks like, her age, hair color, the brands she wears. You know, the important things.

MESSENGER: That sounds very juvenile, almost high school.

CLEOPATRA: JUST DO IT!

MESSENGER: Yes, my queen!

(ALL exit)

ACT 2 SCENE 4

Italy

(POMPEY and his men enter from one side; ANTONY, CAESAR, LEPIDUS, and their men enter from other)

POMPEY: Are you ready to go to battle?

CAESAR: Are you ready to perish here?

LEPIDUS: Yeah, do the math. Three of us. One of you.

ANTONY: But we will make you a deal. You have a choice: die or...

LEPIDUS: OR... we give you Sicily and you must rid all the sea of pirates.

CAESAR: That's our offer. Death or your own private island!

(pause; EVERYONE hums Jeopardy theme)

POMPEY: I'll take the island! *(they all cheer)* Now, aboard my galley I invite you and we'll feast!

(ALL exit cheering)

ACT 3 SCENE 1

Caesar's house

(enter CAESAR, ANTONY, OCTAVIA, ENOBARBUS, and LEPIDUS who stumbles in)

LEPIDUS: *(stumbling)* THAT was an AWESOME party!!!

ENOBARBUS: *(laughing)* Look at you, troubled with the green sickness, yet you still want to party!

LEPIDUS: Who you calling fool?! And... yeah! Woohoo!!!

(OCTAVIA and CAESAR hug)

OCTAVIA: My noble brother!

CAESAR: Farewell, my dearest Octavia. Antony, take good care of her, or you and I will... well, you know.

ANTONY: You insult me.

(LEPIDUS burps, interrupting their conversation)

LEPIDUS: Sorry! Please continue...

CAESAR: I was just saying...

ANTONY: I know what you were saying. Let's go, Octavia.

(ANTONY and OCTAVIA exit)

CAESAR: Farewell!

LEPIDUS: Well, that wasn't awkward or anything. *(pause)* Now let's get back to partying!!! Woohoo!!!

(ALL exit)

ACT 3 SCENE 2

Cleopatra's palace

(enter CLEOPATRA and CHARMIAN; MESSENGER from other side)

CHARMIAN: You're back already?

MESSENGER: It's a short play.

CLEOPATRA: Soooo... tell me, what's she like?

MESSENGER: Well, my queen, she's dull of tongue and dwarfish.

CLEOPATRA: You mean she's short, smelly, and rather plain looking! Yes!

CHARMIAN: Excellent! Antony will be back in no time.

CLEOPATRA: Yay!

(ALL exit)

Antony's house

(enter ANTONY and OCTAVIA)

ANTONY: Your brother's a piece of work!

OCTAVIA: What did he do now?

ANTONY: New wars 'gainst Pompey, and spoke scantly of me. ME! *(strikes a pose)* The Great Antony!

OCTAVIA: What do you want me to do about it?

ANTONY: Go back and spy on your brother for me.

OCTAVIA: So, I have to choose between you or my brother?

ANTONY: Choose wisely, Octavia. *(ANTONY exits)*

OCTAVIA: *(mocking)* Choose wisely. *(aside)* My brother, or my boyfriend? Oy!

(OCTAVIA exits)

(enter ENOBARBUS and EROS)

EROS: Rumor Mill!

ENOBARBUS: What man?!

EROS: Caesar murder'd Pompey.

ENOBARBUS: What?! By himself?

EROS: Nope. He used Lepidus's army, and THEN put Lepidus in jail!

ENOBARBUS: WHAT?! Seriously? A total coup!!!

EROS: Yeah! Now Antony is headed for Italy and Caesar! Revenge!

ENOBARBUS: Nice exposition. This is going to be good!

(ALL exit)

ACT 3 SCENE 5

Caesar's house

(enter CAESAR and AGRIPPA)

AGRIPPA: So, Caesar, how's it going?!

CAESAR: Horrible! Antony is back with Cleopatra sitting in chairs of gold.

AGRIPPA: That bad, huh?

CAESAR: Worse! Now she's absolute queen of Syria, Cyprus, and Lydia!

AGRIPPA: Boy, can't get more troubling than that.

CAESAR: One would think, but now Antony wants some of the lands I conquered from Pompey!!!

AGRIPPA: How rude!

CAESAR: Right!!!

AGRIPPA: Oh look, your sister!

(OCTAVIA enters)

CAESAR: Octavia! *(they hug)* Where's your fanfare? Your trumpeters?!

OCTAVIA: Oh, I don't have any.

CAESAR: What?! Antony's girlfriend, MY SISTER, should have an army for an usher!

OCTAVIA: Well, he sent me to make peace with you.

CAESAR: Oh, my most wronged sister, he's back together with Cleopatra.

OCTAVIA: What?! Noooooo!!! Boo hoo!!! Waaaaah!!!!

CAESAR: Come on, let's go hatch an evil revenge plan!

(ALL exit laughing evilly)

ACT 3 SCENE 6

Antony's camp, Greece

(enter ENOBARBUS and CLEOPATRA)

ENOBARBUS: Why, why, why join Antony in battle? You will be a distraction to him.

CLEOPATRA: Distraction?! *(tosses hair)* I fail to see how I could POSSIBLY be a distraction.

ENOBARBUS: Yeah... you're right. Never mind.

(enter ANTONY and CANIDIUS)

ANTONY: General Canidius, prepare our ships for battle against Caesar.

CLEOPATRA: I have sixty sails at your disposal as well.

CANIDIUS: Our navy will be ready sir, but...

ANTONY: Yes?

CANIDIUS: But, on land, Caesar's army is too strong, he will prevail.

ANTONY: Nonsense!

CLEOPATRA: General, celerity is never more admired than by the negligent.

ANTONY: A good rebuke.

CANIDIUS: Celery? Now is NOT the time to discuss vegetables!

ANTONY: CEL-ER-ITY not Celery!

CANIDIUS: Oh. Where do you get these fancy words?

CLEOPATRA: Shakespeare. It means swiftness. I read books too, you know. I'm not JUST a pretty girl.

CANIDIUS: Okaaay. *(aside)* Still doesn't make sense. On with the battle! *(ALL exit)*

ACT 3 SCENE 7

(stage is split, on one side CAESAR, AGRIPPA, and SOLDIERS; the other ANTONY, CLEOPATRA, CANIDIUS, ENOBARBUS, and their men)

CAESAR: *(to his men)* Strike not by land, till we have done at sea!

AGRIPPA: Yes, sir!

ANTONY: Set our squadrons and proceed accordingly.

CANIDIUS: Yes, sir!

ANTONY: Enobarbus, stand here, look important, and tell the audience what is happening.

ENOBARBUS: Yes, sir!

(center stage a sea battle of ships ensues (toy boats or cardboard cut-outs) between CAESAR, CANIDIUS, ANTONY, and CLEOPATRA all saying "pew-pew!"; ENOBARBUS does play-by-play like sports announcer)

ENOBARBUS: Welcome to the great Battle of Actium! It looks as if Antony and Cleopatra are beating down Caesar and winning the battle!

(CLEOPATRA suddenly turns and leaves the stage)

ENOBARBUS: Oh no! Cleopatra hoists sails and flies!

ANTONY: Hey! Where are you going?!

CLEOPATRA: I don't know! But I'm out of here!

ANTONY: Well then... I guess I'll... I'll leave too!

CANIDIUS: Wait! Where are you going?! Cowards!

(ANTONY follows CLEOPATRA offstage)

ENOBARBUS: Alack, Alack! My eyes did sicken at the sight! Antony and Cleopatra fled, so... I guess Caesar wins!

CAESAR: Yay!!! Boy, that was lucky!

CANIDIUS: What just happened?!

CAESAR: You lost.

CANIDIUS: That's it! Caesar, I render my legions!

CAESAR: Great! Let's go celebrate!

(CANIDIUS, CAESAR, and his men exit cheering; ANTONY reenters)

ANTONY: I'm such a fool!

ENOBARBUS: Yep.

(ENOBARBUS exits; CLEOPATRA enters)

ANTONY: Cleo, how could you make me look like such a fool?

CLEOPATRA: O my lord, forgive my fearful sails! I little thought you would have follow'd.

ANTONY: Of course, I followed! You are my love. My heart was to thy rudder tied by the strings.

CLEOPATRA: Cute. Corny... but cute. I'm so sorry I caused you all this trouble. Forgive me? *(smiles beautifully)*

ANTONY: Of course, I could never be mad at you for long!

CLEOPATRA: Oh goody!

ANTONY: Now, I, The Great Antony, *(poses yet again!)* have to send humble treaties to Caesar.

CLEOPATRA: Again, so sorry!

(ALL exit)

ACT 3 SCENE 8

(enter CAESAR and MESSENGER opposite)

MESSENGER: Sir, I have a message from Antony.

CAESAR: Approach, and speak.

MESSENGER: Sir, it says that Antony begs you to let him live in Egypt, and if not, maybe a little cabin in Athens?

CAESAR: Is that all?

MESSENGER: Uhhh...no sir. Also, can you give Egypt to Cleopatra's heirs?

CAESAR: What! NOOOOO!!! I have no ears to his request.

MESSENGER: What then, sir?

CAESAR: Hmmm... Cleopatra can live as long as she either exiles or executes Antony. Easy-peasy!

MESSENGER: Very well, sir. *(exits)*

CAESAR: I need to lure Cleopatra into accepting my deal. Time to make Antony squirm.

(exits laughing evilly)

ACT 3 SCENE 9

Cleopatra's palace

(enter CLEOPATRA and ENOBARBUS)

CLEOPATRA: I feel guilty about Antony!

ENOBARBUS: You should.

CLEOPATRA: Huh? You're supposed to make me feel better!

ENOBARBUS: Oh, sorry. *(unconvincingly)* It's not your fault?

CLEOPATRA: *(rolls eyes)* Oh wow. Thanks.

(enter ANTONY)

ANTONY: I'm home!

(enter MESSENGER)

MESSENGER: Caesar says, "Ahhh... no."

ANTONY: Fine! Tell him I challenge him sword against sword for all the marbles!

MESSENGER: Sure thing! *(exits)*

ANTONY: I need to practice my sweet sword skills, I was once a great sworder! *(poses)* I shall be again! *(exits)*

(CAESAR enters secretly)

CAESAR: Psst! Psst!

CLEOPATRA: What do you want?

(ANTONY is peeking around and listening to their conversation)

CAESAR: Listen, if you to turn over Antony, I will grant you Egypt.

CLEOPATRA: Really? You think you can manipulate me?

CAESAR: Yeah.

CLEOPATRA: You're right. I never really liked Antony, anyway.

(ANTONY shows shocked face)

CAESAR: Great!

(ANTONY enters)

ANTONY: By Jove that thunders!

(CAESAR runs offstage)

ANTONY: *(screaming)* I can't believe you were going to betray me!

CLEOPATRA: Who? Me?! Couldn't be! I would NEVER betray YOU!!!

ANTONY: *(suddenly calm)* Oh. Ok, then. I am satisfied.

CLEOPATRA: *(aside)* Whew!

ANTONY: You know... Our navy fleet is threatening most sea-like, and our force by land hath nobly held. I will oppose his fate!

CLEOPATRA: That's my brave lord!

(ANTONY and CLEOPATRA exit)

ENOBARBUS: Hmmm... note to self: seems like Antony is going a bit crazy. *(to audience)* Later!

(ALL exit)

ACT 4 SCENE 1

Caesar's camp, Egypt

(enter CAESAR and MESSENGER opposite)

MESSENGER: Caesar, Antony challenges you to personal combat.

(pause; CAESAR laughs hysterically)

CAESAR: You're funny!!! Antony is weak and pathetic. Tell the old ruffian, NO!

(CAESAR exits; ANTONY, EROS, and ENOBARBUS enter opposite)

ANTONY: Well?

MESSENGER: Ummm, sir... they laughed in your face.

ANTONY: WHAT?!

MESSENGER: Sir, Caesar said, 'I have many other ways to die. Laugh at his challenge.' *(laughs until ANTONY pulls sword; MESSENGER runs offstage)*

ANTONY: Then by sea and land I'll fight!

ENOBARBUS: Are you sure you want to do that, sir?

ANTONY: Yes! I will live or die by honour!

EROS: But, sir...

ANTONY: Stop! It's all about my ego! Haply you shall not see me more, or if, a mangled shadow. I deserve my fate.

ENOBARBUS: Wow. How depressing.

ENOBARBUS: Yeah, way to motivate. Woohoo...

ANTONY: Oh, sorry. Well... I'm sure we will all live? *(very unsure)*

ALL: *(very apathetic)* Yay!

(enter CLEOPATRA)

CLEOPATRA: My dearest, I'll help too.

ANTONY: I think you've helped enough. I will be back soon, my love.

EROS: Sir, a thousand soldiers at the port expect you. Well, except Enobarbus.

ANTONY: What? He is standing right here.

ENOBARBUS: Ahhh, yeah... about that... I'm not going to be there.

ANTONY: Why not?

ENOBARBUS: Well, I think you've gone nuts and I am not supporting you anymore. Love you like a brother, but like a brother in a nuthouse. Sorry, bro!

ANTONY: Makes sense, but... that stinks. Gentle adieus, Enobarbus. Take all thy treasure with, as a thank you. Meanwhile... CHARGE!!! *(ANTONY and others runs off stage ready for battle)*

ENOBARBUS: *(to audience)* Well, great, now I feel guilty. So guilty, I will go seek some ditch wherein to die. Let's see... not that ditch... no, not that one... there! That's a good ditch! Bye-bye.

(ENOBARBUS falls over dead)

ACT 4 SCENE 2

Cleopatra's palace

(ANTONY enters; CLEOPATRA enters opposite)

CLEOPATRA: Com'st thou smiling from the war?

ANTONY: I was glorious in battle today! Tomorrow, Caesar will fall!

(poses)

CLEOPATRA: Yay!

ANTONY: I fought as though I did not like mankind! *(pauses)* But I love YOUR kind, Cleo.

CLEOPATRA: Ahhh, you're so cute, Tony!

ANTONY: Yes. Yes, I am. *(poses – kissing biceps)* Let's go celebrate!

(ALL exit)

ACT 4 SCENE 3

Field of battle between camps

(enter ANTONY and EROS)

ANTONY: Caesar will attack us today by sea, but Cleopatra's ships will help us.

EROS: Let's watch the battle from this hill.

ANTONY: Good idea.

EROS: Oh, would you look at that, Cleopatra just surrendered and joined Caesar.

ANTONY: All is lost! The foul Egyptian has betrayed me.

EROS: It looks that way, sir.

ANTONY: Hmmm... well, this certainly stinks!

EROS: Sooooo, what should we do?

ANTONY: Run, Eros. RUN!!! Go now!

EROS: Aghhhh!!!

(EROS runs offstage)

ANTONY: Cleopatra is evil!!! I will be revenged upon my charm.

(CLEOPATRA enters)

ANTONY: Ah, thou spell! Avaunt!

CLEOPATRA: What?!

ANTONY: GET OUT OF HERE!!!

(ANTONY chases CLEOPATRA offstage, both are crazy screaming)

ACT 4 SCENE 4

Cleopatra's palace

(enter CLEOPATRA and CHARMIAN from opposite)

CLEOPATRA: Help me! Oh, he's mad! Crazy, I tell you!

CHARMIAN: Who?

CLEOPATRA: WHO?! Antony, that's who!

CHARMIAN: Why?

CLEOPATRA: I dunno, something about betraying him. I was too busy screaming and running to hear anything.

CHARMIAN: Well, did you betray him?

CLEOPATRA: Who, me? Yeah.

CHARMIAN: I have an idea, why don't you send word that you killed yourself!

CLEOPATRA: Ohhhh, very Romeo and Juliet!

CHARMIAN: Who?

CLEOPATRA: Nevermind, that's still a few hundred years away.

CHARMIAN: Oh.

CLEOPATRA: But, great idea, go tell him I have slain myself!

(ALL exit)

(enter ANTONY and EROS)

ANTONY: Give me my sword, Eros. It is time that I vanquish Cleopatra!

(enter MESSENGER; ANTONY pulls sword on him)

ANTONY: What do you want?

MESSENGER: Woah! Ever heard of the term 'don't kill the messenger'?

ANTONY: Fine! What's your message?

MESSENGER: To tell you Cleopatra killed herself.

ANTONY: WHAT?! NOOOOOOOO!!!!

MESSENGER: Yes. Her last words were, "Antony! Most noble Antony!"

ANTONY: NOOOOOOOO!!!!

MESSENGER: Again, yes. Goodbye. *(exits)*

ANTONY: Eros, I am disgrace and horror. Thou wouldst kill me: do't. *(hands sword to EROS, who drops it)*

EROS: Ewwww, no!

ANTONY: What?! Draw and come.

EROS: Agh! Fine. My sword is drawn. Farewell.

ANTONY: Yes. Farewell.

EROS: Shall I strike now?

ANTONY: Yes, now!

(EROS stabs himself)

EROS: Ok, bye! *(dies)*

ANTONY: What?! O valiant Eros. Thou teaches me. *(stabs self)* How! Not dead? Not dead?!

(MESSENGER enters)

MESSENGER: Antony?

ANTONY: Yeah? *(he falls to knee in pain)*

MESSENGER: Ahh... Cleopatra sent you word she was dead, but... she's not.

ANTONY: What?!

MESSENGER: Surprise!

ANTONY: *(drops to both knees)* Bear me where Cleopatra bides. I am dying, Egypt, dying.

MESSENGER: Ok, but this is a new toga, don't get it all bloody.

(MESSENGER helps ANTONY offstage)

Cleopatra's palace

(enter CLEOPATRA and CHARMIAN; enter ANTONY opposite)

ANTONY: I'm baaack!

CLEOPATRA: Oh, goodie!

ANTONY: But, I'm going to die.

CLEOPATRA: Oh, noooo!

ANTONY: I love you!

CLEOPATRA: I love you!

ANTONY: I love you more!

CLEOPATRA: No! I love you more!

ANTONY: NO! I love... Achhhh... *(poses one last time, then falls over dead)*

CHARMIAN: Hmmm, I think he loved you.

CLEOPATRA: The crown o'th' Earth doth melt. Oh, this is my fault! *(weeping)* I must be with my Antony again.

(CLEOPATRA ugly cries as ALL exit)

ACT 5 SCENE 1

Caesar's camp

(enter CAESAR; MESSENGER from opposite carrying sword)

CAESAR: What are you doing with a sword?

MESSENGER: Antony is dead. This is his sword.

CAESAR: What? How did that happen?

MESSENGER: Well, you see, Cleopatra...

CAESAR: Stop, you've said enough! Who killed him?

MESSENGER: Not by a hired knife, but that self hand who did all the great deeds that Antony is known for!

CAESAR: What?

MESSENGER: He killed himself.

CAESAR: Oh, I see what you did there.

MESSENGER: Clever, huh?

CAESAR: Very. We must mourn such an extraordinary man. The breaking of so great a thing should make a greater crack.

AGRIPPA: Ummm, weren't we just trying to kill him a few scenes ago?

CAESAR: Yeah, but I'm past that. It's now ok to weep for our loss.

AGRIPPA: Okey-dokey, boss!

MESSENGER: Oh, and the queen desires instructions of your intentions.

CAESAR: Bid her have good heart. I plan her no harm.

MESSENGER: Yes, sir. *(exits)*

CAESAR: Actually, I'll parade her through Rome eternal in our triumph! Bwahahaha!!!

AGRIPPA: Wow. You are really evil. Nice!

CAESAR: Thank you, it's one of my better qualities. Go with your speediest to make sure she doesn't spoil my plan!

AGRIPPA: Caesar, I shall!

(ALL exit)

ACT 5 SCENE 2

Alexandria, A monument

(enter CLEOPATRA and CHARMIAN)

CLEOPATRA: I do not trust Caesar.

CHARMIAN: No, you shouldn't. It is best you take matters into your own hands.

(enter AGRIPPA grabs CLEOPATRA)

AGRIPPA: I'll take the queen to my guard until Caesar arrives.

CHARMIAN: What are Caesar's plans?

AGRIPPA: Oh, nothing.

CHARMIAN: Something I'm sure. What, Agrippa?

CHARMIAN: What?!

AGRIPPA: Nothing! Nothing!

CHARMIAN: WHAT!?!?!

AGRIPPA: Okay, okay. He'll lead her in triumph through Rome... FOREVER.

CHARMIAN: Wow. That stinks.

(AGRIPPA goes to side)

CLEOPATRA: Sure does. Not going to let that happen. But, hark thee, Charmian.

CHARMIAN: Yes?

CLEOPATRA: Get the snakes.

CHARMIAN: The asps?! Oh, the good gods! But they'll kill you!

CLEOPATRA: Exactly! Go put it to the haste.

(CHARMIAN exits and returns with snakes)

CHARMIAN: Okay, one for each of us!

AGRIPPA: What are you ladies doing over there?

CHARMIAN & CLEOPATRA: Nothing!

AGRIPPA: Oh good. For a second, I thought you were up to something.

CLEOPATRA: NOW!

(they are bitten and die most melodramatic deaths)

CLEOPATRA: Now no more the juice of Egypt's grape shall moist these lips. *(dies)*

(enter CAESAR)

CAESAR: What's this?!

AGRIPPA: It looks as if they are dead.

CAESAR: No kidding. Bummer, she spoiled all my fun!

AGRIPPA: What shall we do?

CAESAR: She shall be buried by her Antony. As for us...

AGRIPPA: Yes...

CAESAR: We get to rule the world!

(maniacal laugh as ALL exit)

THE END

NOTES

The 20-Minute or so Antony & Cleopatra

By William Shakespeare
Creatively modified by
Brendan P. Kelso

12 - 17 Actors

CAST OF CHARACTERS:

TEAM ANTONY AND CLEOPATRA:

ANTONY: one of the Roman triumvirate and in love with Cleopatra

CLEOPATRA: in love with Antony and ruler of Egypt

[3]**CHARMIAN:** attendant to Cleopatra

[5]**IRAS:** another attendant to Cleopatra

ENOBARBUS: mostly faithful supporter of Antony

EROS: one of Antony's dudes

[4]**CANIDIUS:** general in Antony's military

TEAM CAESAR:

OCTAVIUS CAESAR: Julius' nephew and a member of the triumvirate

LEPIDUS: The third triumvirate (he's not around long)

[5]**OCTAVIA:** Caesar's sister

[2]**AGRIPPA:** one of Caesar's officers

[1]**THIDIAS:** one of the Caesar's dudes

OTHERS:

[1]**POMPEY:** bad guy who wants to cause trouble

[4]**MENAS:** one of Pompey's pirates

[2]**SOLDIER 1:** a soldier

[3]**SOLDIER 2:** another soldier

MESSENGER: a messenger, duh

The same actors can play the following part:

[1]THIDIAS and POMPEY

[2]SOLDIER 1 and AGRIPPA

[3]SOLDIER 2 and CHARMIAN

[4]MENAS and CANIDIUS

[5]IRAS and OCTAVIA

EXTRAS can be soldiers throughout play

ACT 1 SCENE 1

Cleopatra's palace, Egypt

(enter SOLDIER 1 & 2 wearing Egyptian souvenirs)

SOLDIER 1: Those pyramids were awesome!

SOLDIER 2: Totally! Hey, did you read the National Egyptian this morning?

SOLDIER 1: Yes! It said Antony, a ruler of Rome, has totally fallen in love with the Egyptian queen, Cleopatra! Speaking of... here's the strumpet's fool now!

(enter ANTONY and CLEOPATRA)

CLEOPATRA: If it be love indeed, tell me how much.

ANTONY: More than the entire Roman empire!

SOLDIER 2: *(aside)* That's a lot!!!

(enter MESSENGER)

MESSENGER: News, my good lord, from Rome.

ANTONY: *(referencing CLEOPATRA)* Can't you see I'm busy?

CLEOPATRA: *(loving the adoration)* Darling, you really should get back to defending Rome.

ANTONY: Let Rome melt! My duty is you, my love.

CLEOPATRA: You're such a kidder. *(grabs his hand)* Let's go check out the Sphinx!

(ANTONY and CLEOPATRA exit)

SOLDIER 1: *(their mouths agape)* Did you hear what he said about Rome?

SOLDIER 2: Such disrespect!

(ALL exit)

ACT 1 SCENE 2

(enter CHARMIAN and IRAS; CLEOPATRA follows)

CLEOPATRA: Charmian and Iras, men are weird. First, he wants nothing to do with Rome, and now it's "Rome, Rome, Rome"!!! Hmph!!!

(CHARMIAN and IRAS nod emphatically saying snide comments)

CHARMIAN: Madam, here comes Antony.

CLEOPATRA: Well that's my cue to exit, bye-bye!

(CLEOPATRA, CHARMIAN, and IRAS exit; ANTONY and MESSENGER enter opposite)

MESSENGER: Sir, your brother lost his battle against Octavius Caesar.

ANTONY: Well, that's a bummer.

MESSENGER: Sir, you do realize if you would've been there...

(ANTONY glares at him)

ANTONY: Excuse me? Taunt my faults?

MESSENGER: What?! I didn't say anything... must have been him! *(points at audience member; ANTONY double claps – SOLDIERS run on and remove MESSENGER)*

ANTONY: Arghhh! I must be gone to Rome. My people need me! *(turns to leave)*

(CLEOPATRA, CHARMIAN, and IRAS enter)

CLEOPATRA: Oh, Antony.

ANTONY: Yes, my dear?

CLEOPATRA: I'm worried when you leave you will not care for me anymore.

ANTONY: Now, my dearest queen, Rome's really messed up, and they need me, The Great Antony! *(strikes a pose)*

CLEOPATRA: But Rome is so far from Egypt.

ANTONY: My precious queen, distance doesn't matter, because my heart is here. Adieu!

(ALL exit)

ACT 1 SCENE 3

Rome

(enter CAESAR and LEPIDUS)

CAESAR: Lepidus, you, Antony, and I rule Rome. The Triumvirate. Yet he continues to leave. As you can tell I am peeved.

LEPIDUS: Caesar, Antony does like to vacation. A lot. But, he's done a lot of great things, 'tis pity him.

CAESAR: No! Pompey thrives in our idleness and we need Antony here, not in Egypt.

LEPIDUS: Agreed, but he's not here.

CAESAR: Antony is one of the best soldiers ever.

LEPIDUS: Again, yes, but not here.

CAESAR: Antony was always nice to my cat.

LEPIDUS: Ugh, Yes, BUT HE'S NOT HERE! Let's get an army together to fight Pompey.

CAESAR: Fine. Let's go!

(ALL exit)

ACT 1 SCENE 4

Cleopatra's palace

(enter CLEOPATRA, CHARMIAN, and IRAS)

IRAS: I have a gift from Antony. *(presents gift to CLEOPATRA)*

CLEOPATRA: Awww... How pretty! Oh, how I miss Antony!

CHARMIAN: He kiss'd this orient pearl. His way of saying... bye-bye with love.

IRAS & CHARMIAN: Awwww.

CLEOPATRA: I know. *(melodramatically)* I will write him a love letter. EVERY. SINGLE. DAY!

IRAS: A bit smothering, don't ya think?

CLEOPATRA: No. That's loooove! How about this one... O happy horse, to bear the weight of Antony! *(melodramatically)* Eternity was in our lips and in our eyes.

CHARMIAN: Wow, totally gross. Come on, you lovesick fool!

(ALL exit)

ACT 2 SCENE 1

Pompey's house, Italy

(enter POMPEY and MENAS)

POMPEY: Come here Menas, my faithful lieutenant.

MENAS: Yes, sir!

POMPEY: We are about to go into battle against the triumvirate.

MENAS: That will be three against one, sir! How are we ever going to win?!

POMPEY: You see, I control the sea, and Mark Antony, their greatest leader, in Egypt sits at dinner. Victory shall be mine!

MENAS: Ummm, sir? I hear Caesar and Lepidus have recruited an army against you.

POMPEY: Well, that's a problem! *(enter MESSENGER)* How now messenger?!

MESSENGER: Sir. Antony is in Rome, expected.

POMPEY: Well, double poop! My nefarious plans are dwindling with each line of this play! Time to think of another dastardly plan! Men, let's go!

ALL: Yes, sir!

(ALL exit, MESSENGER shrugs to audience and marches out with others)

ACT 2 SCENE 2

House of Lepidus, Rome

(enter ANTONY and LEPIDUS from one side; CAESAR and AGRIPPA from other)

LEPIDUS: Please use soft and gentle speech with Caesar.

ANTONY: I shall use as hard and honest words as I feel.

(CAESAR and ANTONY meet at center, ANTONY strikes a pose)

CAESAR: Sit.

ANTONY: No. You sit, sir.

CAESAR: Nay, then. I should say myself offended. Your being in Egypt, while we need your military support. Specifically, me!

ANTONY: Caesar, look at you, you're very talented and don't need me!

CAESAR: *(unsuccessfully trying to pose like ANTONY)* I KNOW THAT! But... that doesn't matter! You should be here, not gallivanting around Egypt!

LEPIDUS: Men! Stop bickering. Time calls upon's: Of us must Pompey presently be sought.

ANTONY & CAESAR: Huh?

LEPIDUS: You know... our looming battle.

(they reluctantly nod in agreement)

AGRIPPA: Give me leave, Caesar.

CAESAR: Speak, Agrippa.

AGRIPPA: Antony, why don't you date Caesar's sister? Then it's all in the family, and you will prove your allegiance.

CAESAR: Yeah? What do you say... Brother?

ANTONY: Date her? *(aside)* It's a smart political move. BUT, Cleopatra will NOT be happy. BUT, I should stay faithful to Rome. BUT, I'm sure Cleopatra would totally understand, right? I mean, what could possibly go wrong? *(to CAESAR)* Let's do it!

(they shake hands)

CAESAR: Great! Now let's go take on Pompey!

ANTONY: One for all!

CAESAR and LEPIDUS: And all for one!

(ALL exit)

Cleopatra's palace

(enter CLEOPATRA and MESSENGER, opposite)

MESSENGER: Madam, a message about Antony.

CLEOPATRA: *(melodramatically overreacting)* What?! Oh no!!! Antonius dead!!!

MESSENGER: No, no. He's well, but yet...

CLEOPATRA: I do not like, 'but yet'. But yet could mean a lot of things! But yet he is dead! *(ugly cries)*

MESSENGER: Madam, he is well... just... dating someone.

CLEOPATRA: WHAT?! Ohhh... he's going to wish he were dead!!!

MESSENGER: Okayyyy, on that note, I'm outta here! *(exits frantically)*

CLEOPATRA: No wait! *(MESSENGER returns, scared)*

MESSENGER: Y-Y-Yes.

CLEOPATRA: Go back and spy on her. Tell me what she looks like, her age, hair color, the brands she wears. You know, the important things.

MESSENGER: That sounds very juvenile, almost high school.

CLEOPATRA: JUST DO IT!

MESSENGER: Yes, my queen!

(ALL exit)

ACT 2 SCENE 4

Italy

(POMPEY and his men enter from one side; ANTONY, CAESAR, LEPIDUS, and their men enter from other)

POMPEY: Are you ready to go to battle?

CAESAR: Are you ready to perish here?

LEPIDUS: Yeah, do the math. Three of us. One of you.

ANTONY: But we will make you a deal. You have a choice: die or...

LEPIDUS: OR... we give you Sicily and you must rid all the sea of pirates.

CAESAR: That's our offer. Death or your own private island!

(pause; EVERYONE hums Jeopardy theme)

POMPEY: I'll take the island! *(they all cheer)* Now, aboard my galley I invite you and we'll feast!

(ALL exit cheering)

ACT 3 SCENE 1

Caesar's house

(enter CAESAR, ANTONY, OCTAVIA, AGRIPPA, ENOBARBUS, and LEPIDUS who stumbles in)

LEPIDUS: *(stumbling)* THAT was an AWESOME party!!!

AGRIPPA: *(laughing)* Look at him!

ENOBARBUS: The fool is troubled with the green sickness, yet still wants to party!

LEPIDUS: Who you calling fool?! And... yeah! Woohoo!!!

(OCTAVIA and CAESAR hug)

OCTAVIA: My noble brother!

CAESAR: Farewell, my dearest Octavia. Antony, take good care of her, or you and I will... well, you know.

ANTONY: You insult me.

(LEPIDUS burps, interrupting their conversation)

LEPIDUS: Sorry! Please continue...

CAESAR: I was just saying...

ANTONY: I know what you were saying. Let's go, Octavia.

(ANTONY and OCTAVIA exit)

CAESAR: Farewell!

LEPIDUS: Well, that wasn't awkward or anything. *(pause)* Now let's get back to partying!!! Woohoo!!!

(ALL exit)

ACT 3 SCENE 2

Cleopatra's palace

(enter CLEOPATRA and CHARMIAN; MESSENGER from other side)

CHARMIAN: You're back already?

MESSENGER: It's a short play.

CLEOPATRA: Soooo... tell me, what's she like?

MESSENGER: Well, my queen, she's dull of tongue and dwarfish.

CLEOPATRA: You mean she's short, smelly, and rather plain looking! Yes!

CHARMIAN: Excellent! Antony will be back in no time.

CLEOPATRA: Yay!

(ALL exit)

ACT 3 SCENE 3

Antony's house

(enter ANTONY and OCTAVIA)

ANTONY: Your brother's a piece of work!

OCTAVIA: What did he do now?

ANTONY: New wars 'gainst Pompey, and spoke scantly of me. ME! *(strikes a pose)* The Great Antony!

OCTAVIA: What do you want me to do about it?

ANTONY: Go back and spy on your brother for me.

OCTAVIA: So, I have to choose between you or my brother?

ANTONY: Choose wisely, Octavia. *(ANTONY exits)*

OCTAVIA: *(mocking)* Choose wisely. *(aside)* My brother, or my boyfriend? Oy!

(OCTAVIA exits)

(enter ENOBARBUS and EROS)

EROS: Rumor Mill!

ENOBARBUS: What man?!

EROS: Caesar murder'd Pompey.

ENOBARBUS: What?! By himself?

EROS: Nope. He used Lepidus's army, and THEN put Lepidus in jail!

ENOBARBUS: WHAT?! Seriously? A total coup!!!

EROS: Yeah! Now Antony is headed for Italy and Caesar! Revenge!

ENOBARBUS: Nice exposition. This is going to be good!

(POMPEY enters)

POMPEY: Wait a minute... did I just hear you say that I'm dead?

ENOBARBUS: That be true, sir!

POMPEY: Darn! Well, that stinks! *(dies melodramatically)*

EROS: Such overactors...

ENOBARBUS: Right?

(ALL exit)

ACT 3 SCENE 5

Caesar's house

(enter CAESAR and AGRIPPA)

AGRIPPA: So, Caesar, how's it going?!

CAESAR: Horrible! Antony is back with Cleopatra sitting in chairs of gold.

AGRIPPA: That bad, huh?

CAESAR: Worse! Now she's absolute queen of Syria, Cyprus, and Lydia!

AGRIPPA: Boy, can't get more troubling than that.

CAESAR: One would think, but now Antony wants some of the lands I conquered from Pompey!!!

AGRIPPA: How rude!

CAESAR: Right!!!

AGRIPPA: Oh look, your sister!

(OCTAVIA enters)

CAESAR: Octavia! *(they hug)* Where's your fanfare? Your trumpeters?!

OCTAVIA: Oh, I don't have any.

CAESAR: What?! Antony's girlfriend, MY SISTER, should have an army for an usher!

OCTAVIA: Well, he sent me to make peace with you.

CAESAR: Oh, my most wronged sister, he's back together with Cleopatra.

OCTAVIA: What?! Noooooo!!! Boo hoo!!! Waaaaah!!!!

CAESAR: Come on, let's go hatch an evil revenge plan!

(ALL exit laughing evilly)

ACT 3 SCENE 6

Antony's camp, Greece

(enter ENOBARBUS and CLEOPATRA)

ENOBARBUS: Why, why, why join Antony in battle? You will be a distraction to him.

CLEOPATRA: Distraction?! *(tosses hair)* I fail to see how I could POSSIBLY be a distraction.

ENOBARBUS: Yeah... you're right. Never mind.

(enter ANTONY and CANIDIUS)

ANTONY: General Canidius, prepare our ships for battle against Caesar.

CLEOPATRA: I have sixty sails at your disposal as well.

CANIDIUS: Our navy will be ready sir, but...

ANTONY: Yes?

CANIDIUS: But, on land, Caesar's army is too strong, he will prevail.

ANTONY: Nonsense!

CLEOPATRA: General, celerity is never more admired than by the negligent.

ANTONY: A good rebuke.

CANIDIUS: Celery? Now is NOT the time to discuss vegetables!

ANTONY: CEL-ER-ITY not Celery!

CANIDIUS: Oh. Where do you get these fancy words?

CLEOPATRA: Shakespeare. It means swiftness. I read books too, you know. I'm not JUST a pretty girl.

CANIDIUS: Okaaay. *(aside)* Still doesn't make sense. On with the battle! *(ALL exit)*

ACT 3 SCENE 7

(stage is split, on one side CAESAR, AGRIPPA, and his SOLDIERS; the other ANTONY, CLEOPATRA, CANIDIUS, ENOBARBUS, and their men)

CAESAR: *(to his men)* Strike not by land, till we have done at sea!

SOLDIERS: Yes, sir!

ANTONY: Set our squadrons and proceed accordingly.

CANIDIUS: Yes, sir!

ANTONY: Enobarbus, stand here, look important, and tell the audience what is happening.

ENOBARBUS: Yes, sir!

(center stage a sea battle of ships ensues (toy boats or cardboard cut-outs) between CAESAR, CANIDIUS, ANTONY, and CLEOPATRA all saying "pew-pew!"; ENOBARBUS does play-by-play like sports announcer)

ENOBARBUS: Welcome to the great Battle of Actium! It looks as if Antony and Cleopatra are beating down Caesar and winning the battle!

(CLEOPATRA suddenly turns and leaves the stage)

ENOBARBUS: Oh no! Cleopatra hoists sails and flies!

ANTONY: Hey! Where are you going?!

CLEOPATRA: I don't know! But I'm out of here!

ANTONY: Well then... I guess I'll... I'll leave too!

CANIDIUS: Wait! Where are you going?! Cowards!

(ANTONY follows CLEOPATRA offstage)

ENOBARBUS: Alack, Alack! My eyes did sicken at the sight! Antony and Cleopatra fled, so... I guess Caesar wins!

CAESAR: Yay!!! Boy, that was lucky!

CANIDIUS: What just happened?!

CAESAR: You lost.

CANIDIUS: That's it! Caesar, I render my legions!

CAESAR: Great! Let's go celebrate!

(CANIDIUS, CAESAR, and his men exit cheering; ANTONY reenters)

ANTONY: I'm such a fool!

ENOBARBUS: Yep.

(ENOBARBUS exits; CLEOPATRA enters)

ANTONY: Cleo, how could you make me look like such a fool?

CLEOPATRA: O my lord, forgive my fearful sails! I little thought you would have follow'd.

ANTONY: Of course, I followed! You are my love. My heart was to thy rudder tied by the strings.

CLEOPATRA: Cute. Corny... but cute. I'm so sorry I caused you all this trouble. Forgive me? *(smiles beautifully)*

ANTONY: Of course, I could never be mad at you for long!

CLEOPATRA: Oh goody!

ANTONY: Now, I, The Great Antony, *(poses yet again!)* have to send humble treaties to Caesar.

CLEOPATRA: Again, so sorry! *(ALL exit)*

ACT 3 SCENE 8

(enter CAESAR and THIDIAS; MESSENGER opposite)

MESSENGER: Sir, I have a message from Antony.

CAESAR: Approach, and speak.

MESSENGER: Sir, it says that Antony begs you to let him live in Egypt, and if not, maybe a little cabin in Athens?

CAESAR: Is that all?

MESSENGER: Uhhh...no sir. Also, can you give Egypt to Cleopatra's heirs?

CAESAR: What! NOOOOO!!! I have no ears to his request.

MESSENGER: What then, sir?

CAESAR: Hmmm... Cleopatra can live as long as she either exiles or executes Antony. Easy-peasy!

MESSENGER: Very well, sir. *(exits)*

CAESAR: Thidias, lure Cleopatra into accepting my deal. Time to make Antony squirm.

THIDIAS: Caesar, I shall!

(ALL exit laughing evilly)

ACT 3 SCENE 9

Cleopatra's palace

(enter CLEOPATRA and ENOBARBUS)

CLEOPATRA: I feel guilty about Antony!

ENOBARBUS: You should.

CLEOPATRA: Huh? You're supposed to make me feel better!

ENOBARBUS: Oh, sorry. *(unconvincingly)* It's not your fault?

CLEOPATRA: *(rolls eyes)* Oh wow. Thanks.

(enter ANTONY)

ANTONY: I'm home!

(enter MESSENGER)

MESSENGER: Caesar says, "Ahhh... no."

ANTONY: Fine! Tell him I challenge him sword against sword for all the marbles!

MESSENGER: Sure thing! *(exits)*

ANTONY: I need to practice my sweet sword skills, I was once a great sworder! *(poses)* I shall be again! *(exits)*

(THIDIAS enters secretly)

THIDIAS: Psst! Psst!

CLEOPATRA: What do you want?

(ANTONY is peeking around and listening to their conversation)

THIDIAS: Caesar asks you to turn over Antony and he will grant you Egypt.

CLEOPATRA: Really? You think you can manipulate me?

THIDIAS: Yeah.

CLEOPATRA: You're right. I never really liked Antony, anyway.

(ANTONY shows shocked face)

THIDIAS: Great!

CLEOPATRA: Tell Caesar he is a god!

(ANTONY enters with SOLDIERS)

ANTONY: By Jove that thunders! *(ANTONY beats up THIDIAS)* Take him to the dungeon!

SOLDIER 1: We have a dungeon?

SOLDIER 2: *(shrugs)* Don't know. But don't ask. Antony is NOT in the mood!

SOLDIER 1: Ok. Let's just take him backstage.

SOLDIER 2: Good idea!

(SOLDIERS take THIDIAS away)

ANTONY: *(screaming)* I can't believe you were going to betray me!

CLEOPATRA: Who? Me?! Couldn't be! I would NEVER betray YOU!!!

ANTONY: *(suddenly calm)* Oh. Ok, then. I am satisfied.

CLEOPATRA: *(aside)* Whew!

ANTONY: You know... Our navy fleet is threatening most sea-like, and our force by land hath nobly held. I will oppose his fate!

CLEOPATRA: That's my brave lord!

(ANTONY and CLEOPATRA exit)

ENOBARBUS: Hmmm... note to self: seems like Antony is going a bit crazy. *(to audience)* Later!

(ALL exit)

ACT 4 SCENE 1

(enter CAESAR and MESSENGER opposite)

MESSENGER: Caesar, Antony challenges you to personal combat.

(pause; CAESAR laughs hysterically)

CAESAR: You're funny!!! Antony is weak and pathetic. Tell the old ruffian, NO!

(CAESAR exits; ANTONY, EROS, ENOBARBUS, and SOLDIERS enter opposite)

ANTONY: Well?

MESSENGER: Ummm, sir... they laughed in your face.

ANTONY: WHAT?!

MESSENGER: Sir, Caesar said, 'I have many other ways to die. Laugh at his challenge.' *(laughs until ANTONY pulls sword; MESSENGER runs offstage)*

ANTONY: Then by sea and land I'll fight!

SOLDIER 2: Are you sure you want to do that, sir?

ANTONY: Yes! I will live or die by honour!

SOLDIER 1: But, sir...

ANTONY: Stop! It's all about my ego! Haply you shall not see me more, or if, a mangled shadow. I deserve my fate.

SOLDIER 2: Wow. How depressing.

ENOBARBUS: Yeah, way to motivate. Woohoo...

ANTONY: Oh, sorry. Well... I'm sure we will all live? *(very unsure)*

ALL: *(very apathetic)* Yay!

(enter CLEOPATRA)

CLEOPATRA: My dearest, I'll help too.

ANTONY: I think you've helped enough. I will be back soon, my love.

EROS: Sir, a thousand soldiers at the port expect you. Well, except Enobarbus.

ANTONY: What? He is standing right here.

ENOBARBUS: Ahhh, yeah... about that... I'm not going to be there.

ANTONY: Why not?

ENOBARBUS: Well, I think you've gone nuts and I am not supporting you anymore. Love you like a brother, but like a brother in a nuthouse. Sorry, bro!

ANTONY: Makes sense, but... that stinks. Gentle adieus, Enobarbus. Take all thy treasure with, as a thank you. Eros, Are you ready?

EROS: Yes, sir.

ANTONY: Great, then lead the way.

EROS: Yes, sir! You heard him, men. Charge!!!

(ALL exit, with ANTONY following; ENOBARBUS remains)

ENOBARBUS: *(to audience)* Well, great, now I feel guilty. So guilty, I will go seek some ditch wherein to die. Let's see... not that ditch... no, not that one... there! That's a good ditch! Bye-bye.

(ENOBARBUS falls over dead)

(ANTONY enters; CLEOPATRA enters opposite)

CLEOPATRA: Com'st thou smiling from the war?

ANTONY: I was glorious in battle today! Tomorrow, Caesar will fall!

(poses)

CLEOPATRA: Yay!

ANTONY: I fought as though I did not like mankind! *(pauses)* But I love YOUR kind, Cleo.

CLEOPATRA: Ahhh, you're so cute, Tony!

ANTONY: Yes. Yes, I am. *(poses – kissing biceps)* Let's go celebrate!

(ALL exit)

ACT 4 SCENE 3

Field of battle between camps

(enter ANTONY and EROS)

ANTONY: Caesar will attack us today by sea, but Cleopatra's ships will help us.

EROS: Let's watch the battle from this hill.

ANTONY: Good idea.

EROS: Oh, would you look at that, Cleopatra just surrendered and joined Caesar.

ANTONY: All is lost! The foul Egyptian has betrayed me.

EROS: It looks that way, sir.

ANTONY: Hmmm... well, this certainly stinks!

EROS: Sooooo, what should we do?

ANTONY: Run, Eros. RUN!!! Go now!

EROS: Aghhhh!!!

(EROS runs offstage)

ANTONY: Cleopatra is evil!!! I will be revenged upon my charm.

(CLEOPATRA enters)

ANTONY: Ah, thou spell! Avaunt!

CLEOPATRA: What?!

ANTONY: GET OUT OF HERE!!!

(ANTONY chases CLEOPATRA offstage, both are crazy screaming)

Cleopatra's palace

(enter CLEOPATRA, IRAS, and CHARMIAN from opposite)

CLEOPATRA: Help me, my women! Oh, he's mad! Crazy, I tell you!

CHARMIAN: Who?

CLEOPATRA: WHO?! Antony, that's who!

IRAS: Why?

CLEOPATRA: I dunno, something about betraying him. I was too busy screaming and running to hear anything.

IRAS: Well, did you betray him?

CLEOPATRA: Who, me? Yeah.

CHARMIAN: I have an idea, why don't you send word that you killed yourself!

CLEOPATRA: Ohhhh, very Romeo and Juliet!

CHARMIAN: Who?

CLEOPATRA: Nevermind, that's still a few hundred years away.

CHARMIAN: Oh.

CLEOPATRA: But, great idea, go tell him I have slain myself!

(ALL exit)

(enter ANTONY and EROS)

ANTONY: Give me my sword, Eros. It is time that I vanquish Cleopatra!

(enter MESSENGER; ANTONY pulls sword on him)

ANTONY: What do you want?

MESSENGER: Woah! Ever heard of the term 'don't kill the messenger'?

ANTONY: Fine! What's your message?

MESSENGER: To tell you Cleopatra killed herself.

ANTONY: WHAT?! NOOOOOOOO!!!!

MESSENGER: Yes. Her last words were, "Antony! Most noble Antony!"

ANTONY: NOOOOOOOO!!!!

MESSENGER: Again, yes. Goodbye. *(exits)*

ANTONY: Eros, I am disgrace and horror. Thou wouldst kill me: do't. *(hands sword to EROS, who drops it)*

EROS: Ewwww, no!

ANTONY: What?! Draw and come.

EROS: Agh! Fine. My sword is drawn. Farewell.

ANTONY: Yes. Farewell.

EROS: Shall I strike now?

ANTONY: Yes, now!

(EROS stabs himself)

EROS: Ok, bye! *(dies)*

ANTONY: What?! O valiant Eros. Thou teaches me. *(stabs self)* How! Not dead? Not dead?!

(MESSENGER enters)

MESSENGER: Antony?

ANTONY: Yeah? *(he falls to knee in pain)*

MESSENGER: Ahh... Cleopatra sent you word she was dead, but... she's not.

ANTONY: What?!

MESSENGER: Surprise!

ANTONY: *(drops to both knees)* Bear me where Cleopatra bides. I am dying, Egypt, dying.

MESSENGER: Ok, but this is a new toga, don't get it all bloody.

(MESSENGER helps ANTONY offstage)

ACT 4 SCENE 6

Cleopatra's palace

(enter CLEOPATRA, CHARMIAN, and IRAS; enter ANTONY opposite)

ANTONY: I'm baaack!

CLEOPATRA: Oh, goodie!

ANTONY: But, I'm going to die.

CLEOPATRA: Oh, noooo!

ANTONY: I love you!

CLEOPATRA: I love you!

ANTONY: I love you more!

CLEOPATRA: No! I love you more!

ANTONY: NO! I love... Achhhh... *(poses one last time, then falls over dead)*

IRAS: Hmmm, I think he loved you.

CLEOPATRA: The crown o'th' Earth doth melt. Oh, this is my fault! *(weeping)* I must be with my Antony again.

(ugly cries as ALL exit)

Caesar's camp

(enter CAESAR and AGRIPPA; MESSENGER from opposite carrying sword)

CAESAR: What are you doing with a sword?

MESSENGER: Antony is dead. This is his sword.

CAESAR: What? How did that happen?

MESSENGER: Well, you see, Cleopatra...

CAESAR: Stop, you've said enough! Who killed him?

MESSENGER: Not by a hired knife, but that self hand who did all the great deeds that Antony is known for!

CAESAR: What?

MESSENGER: He killed himself.

CAESAR: Oh, I see what you did there.

MESSENGER: Clever, huh?

CAESAR: Very. We must mourn such an extraordinary man. The breaking of so great a thing should make a greater crack.

AGRIPPA: Ummm, weren't we just trying to kill him a few scenes ago?

CAESAR: Yeah, but I'm past that. It's now ok to weep for our loss.

AGRIPPA: Okey-dokey, boss!

MESSENGER: Oh, and the queen desires instructions of your intentions.

CAESAR: Bid her have good heart. I plan her no harm.

MESSENGER: Yes, sir. *(exits)*

CAESAR: Actually, I'll parade her through Rome eternal in our triumph! Bwahahaha!!!

AGRIPPA: Wow. You are really evil. Nice!

CAESAR: Thank you, it's one of my better qualities. Go with your speediest to make sure she doesn't spoil my plan!

AGRIPPA: Caesar, I shall!

(ALL exit)

ACT 5 SCENE 2

Alexandria, A monument

(enter CLEOPATRA, IRAS, and CHARMIAN)

CLEOPATRA: Ladies, I do not trust Caesar.

CHARMIAN: No, you shouldn't. It is best you take matters into your own hands.

(enter AGRIPPA grabs CLEOPATRA)

AGRIPPA: I'll take the queen to my guard until Caesar arrives.

IRAS: What are Caesar's plans?

AGRIPPA: Oh, nothing.

CHARMIAN: Something I'm sure. What, Agrippa?

IRAS: What?!

AGRIPPA: Nothing! Nothing!

IRAS & CHARMIAN: WHAT!?!?!

AGRIPPA: Okay, okay. He'll lead her in triumph through Rome... FOREVER.

IRAS: Wow.

CHARMIAN: That stinks.

(AGRIPPA goes to side)

CLEOPATRA: Sure does. Not going to let that happen. But, hark thee, Charmian and Iras.

CHARMIAN & IRAS: Yes?

CLEOPATRA: Get the snakes.

IRAS: The asps?! Oh, the good gods! But they'll kill you!

CLEOPATRA: Exactly! Go put it to the haste.

(CHARMIAN exits and returns with snakes)

CHARMIAN: Okay, one for each of us!

AGRIPPA: What are you ladies doing over there?

CHARMIAN, IRAS, & CLEOPATRA: Nothing!

AGRIPPA: Oh good. For a second, I thought you were up to something.

CLEOPATRA: NOW!

(all three are bitten and die most melodramatic deaths)

CLEOPATRA: Now no more the juice of Egypt's grape shall moist these lips. *(dies)*

(enter CAESAR)

CAESAR: What's this?!

AGRIPPA: It looks as if they are dead.

CAESAR: No kidding. Bummer, she spoiled all my fun!

AGRIPPA: What shall we do?

CAESAR: She shall be buried by her Antony. As for us...

AGRIPPA: Yes...

CAESAR: We get to rule the world!

(maniacal laugh as ALL exit)

THE END

The 25-Minute or so
Antony & Cleopatra
By William Shakespeare
Creatively modified by
Brendan P. Kelso

15 - 22+ Actors

CAST OF CHARACTERS:

TEAM ANTONY AND CLEOPATRA:

ANTONY: one of the Roman triumvirate and in love with Cleopatra

CLEOPATRA: in love with Antony and ruler of Egypt

CHARMIAN: attendant to Cleopatra

IRAS: another attendant to Cleopatra

[5]**ENOBARBUS:** mostly faithful supporter of Antony

[3]**EROS:** one of Antony's dudes

[1]**SCARUS:** a young soldier of Antony's

[5]**DIOMEDES:** servant of Cleopatra

[4]**CANIDIUS:** general in Antony's military

TEAM CAESAR:

OCTAVIUS CAESAR: Julius' nephew and a member of the triumvirate

[2]**LEPIDUS:** The third triumvirate (he's not around long)

OCTAVIA: Caesar's sister

AGRIPPA: one of Caesar's officers

[1]**THIDIAS:** one of the Caesar's dudes

[2]**DOLABELLA:** Caesar supporter

[4]**MAECENAS:** an officer of Caesar's

OTHERS:

¹POMPEY: bad guy who wants to cause trouble

³MENECRATES: Pompey's pirate officer

⁴MENAS: another Pompey pirate

SOLDIER 1: a soldier

SOLDIER 2: another soldier

MESSENGER: a messenger, duh

The same actors can play the following part:

¹SCARUS, THIDIAS, and POMPEY

²LEPIDUS and DOLABELLA

³EROS and MENECRATES

⁴MENAS, MAECENAS, and CANIDIUS

⁵DIOMEDES and ENOBARBUS

EXTRAS can be soldiers throughout play

ACT 1 SCENE 1

Cleopatra's palace, Egypt

(enter SOLDIER 1 & 2 wearing Egyptian souvenirs)

SOLDIER 1: Those pyramids were awesome!

SOLDIER 2: Totally! Hey, did you read the National Egyptian this morning?

SOLDIER 1: Yes! It said Antony, a ruler of Rome, has totally fallen in love with the Egyptian queen, Cleopatra! Speaking of... here's the strumpet's fool now!

(enter ANTONY and CLEOPATRA)

CLEOPATRA: If it be love indeed, tell me how much.

ANTONY: More than the entire Roman empire!

SOLDIER 2: *(aside)* That's a lot!!!

(enter MESSENGER)

MESSENGER: News, my good lord, from Rome.

ANTONY: *(referencing CLEOPATRA)* Can't you see I'm busy?

CLEOPATRA: *(loving the adoration)* Darling, you really should get back to defending Rome.

ANTONY: Let Rome melt! My duty is you, my love.

CLEOPATRA: You're such a kidder. *(grabs his hand)* Let's go check out the Sphinx!

(ANTONY and CLEOPATRA exit)

SOLDIER 1: *(their mouths agape)* Did you hear what he said about Rome?

SOLDIER 2: Such disrespect!

(ALL exit)

PlayingWithPlays.com

(enter CHARMIAN and IRAS; CLEOPATRA follows)

CLEOPATRA: Charmian and Iras, men are weird. First, he wants nothing to do with Rome, and now it's "Rome, Rome, Rome"!!! Hmph!!!

(CHARMIAN and IRAS nod emphatically saying snide comments)

CHARMIAN: Madam, here comes Antony.

CLEOPATRA: Well that's my cue to exit, bye-bye!

(CLEOPATRA, CHARMIAN, and IRAS exit; ANTONY and MESSENGER enter opposite)

MESSENGER: Sir, your brother lost his battle against Octavius Caesar.

ANTONY: Well, that's a bummer.

MESSENGER: Sir, you do realize if you would've been there...

(ANTONY glares at him)

ANTONY: Excuse me? Taunt my faults?

MESSENGER: What?! I didn't say anything... must have been him! *(points at audience member; ANTONY double claps – SOLDIERS run on and remove MESSENGER)*

ANTONY: Arghhh! I must be gone to Rome. My people need me! *(turns to leave)*

(CLEOPATRA, CHARMIAN, and IRAS enter)

CLEOPATRA: Oh, Antony.

ANTONY: Yes, my dear?

CLEOPATRA: I'm worried when you leave you will not care for me anymore.

ANTONY: Now, my dearest queen, Rome's really messed up, and they need me, The Great Antony! *(strikes a pose)*

CLEOPATRA: But Rome is so far from Egypt.

ANTONY: My precious queen, distance doesn't matter, because my heart is here. Adieu!

(ALL exit)

ACT 1 SCENE 3

(enter CAESAR and LEPIDUS)

CAESAR: Lepidus, you, Antony, and I rule Rome. The Triumvirate. Yet he continues to leave. As you can tell I am peeved.

LEPIDUS: Caesar, Antony does like to vacation. A lot. But, he's done a lot of great things, 'tis pity him.

CAESAR: No! Pompey thrives in our idleness and we need Antony here, not in Egypt.

LEPIDUS: Agreed, but he's not here.

CAESAR: Antony is one of the best soldiers ever.

LEPIDUS: Again, yes, but not here.

CAESAR: Antony was always nice to my cat.

LEPIDUS: Ugh, Yes, BUT HE'S NOT HERE! Let's get an army together to fight Pompey.

CAESAR: Fine. Let's go!

(ALL exit)

ACT 1 SCENE 4

Cleopatra's palace

(enter CLEOPATRA, CHARMIAN, and IRAS)

IRAS: I have a gift from Antony. *(presents gift to CLEOPATRA)*

CLEOPATRA: Awww... How pretty! Oh, how I miss Antony!

CHARMIAN: He kiss'd this orient pearl. His way of saying... bye-bye with love.

IRAS & CHARMIAN: Awwww.

CLEOPATRA: I know. *(melodramatically)* I will write him a love letter. EVERY. SINGLE. DAY!

IRAS: A bit smothering, don't ya think?

CLEOPATRA: No. That's loooove! How about this one... O happy horse, to bear the weight of Antony! *(melodramatically)* Eternity was in our lips and in our eyes.

CHARMIAN: Wow, totally gross. Come on, you lovesick fool!

(ALL exit)

ACT 2 SCENE 1

Pompey's house, Italy

(enter POMPEY, MENECRATES, and MENAS)

POMPEY: Come here Menecrates and Menas, my faithful lieutenants.

MENECRATES & MENAS: Yes, sir!

POMPEY: We are about to go into battle against the triumvirate.

MENECRATES: That will be three against one, sir!

MENAS: How are we ever going to win?!

POMPEY: Men... I control the sea, and Mark Antony, their greatest leader, in Egypt sits at dinner. Victory shall be mine!

MENECRATES: Ummm, sir? I hear Caesar and Lepidus have recruited an army against you.

POMPEY: Well, that's a problem! *(enter MESSENGER)* How now messenger?!

MESSENGER: Sir. Antony is in Rome, expected.

POMPEY: Well, double poop! My nefarious plans are dwindling with each line of this play! Time to think of another dastardly plan! Men, let's go!

ALL: Yes, sir!

(ALL exit, marching)

ACT 2 SCENE 2

House of Lepidus, Rome

(enter ANTONY and LEPIDUS from one side; CAESAR and AGRIPPA from other)

LEPIDUS: Please use soft and gentle speech with Caesar.

ANTONY: I shall use as hard and honest words as I feel.

(CAESAR and ANTONY meet at center, ANTONY strikes a pose)

CAESAR: Sit.

ANTONY: No. You sit, sir.

CAESAR: Nay, then. I should say myself offended. Your being in Egypt, while we need your military support. Specifically, me!

ANTONY: Caesar, look at you, you're very talented and don't need me!

CAESAR: *(unsuccessfully trying to pose like ANTONY)* I KNOW THAT! But... that doesn't matter! You should be here, not gallivanting around Egypt!

LEPIDUS: Men! Stop bickering. Time calls upon's: Of us must Pompey presently be sought.

ANTONY & CAESAR: Huh?

LEPIDUS: You know... our looming battle.

(they reluctantly nod in agreement)

AGRIPPA: Give me leave, Caesar.

CAESAR: Speak, Agrippa.

AGRIPPA: Antony, why don't you date Caesar's sister? Then it's all in the family, and you will prove your allegiance.

CAESAR: Yeah? What do you say... Brother?

ANTONY: Date her? *(aside)* It's a smart political move. BUT, Cleopatra will NOT be happy. BUT, I should stay faithful to Rome. BUT, I'm sure Cleopatra would totally understand, right? I mean, what could possibly go wrong? *(to CAESAR)* Let's do it!

(they shake hands)

CAESAR: Great! Now let's go take on Pompey!

ANTONY: One for all!

CAESAR and LEPIDUS: And all for one!

(ALL exit)

ACT 2 SCENE 3

Cleopatra's palace

(enter CLEOPATRA and MESSENGER, opposite)

MESSENGER: Madam, a message about Antony.

CLEOPATRA: *(melodramatically overreacting)* What?! Oh no!!! Antonius dead!!!

MESSENGER: No, no. He's well, but yet...

CLEOPATRA: I do not like, 'but yet'. But yet could mean a lot of things! But yet he is dead! *(ugly cries)*

MESSENGER: Madam, he is well... just... dating someone.

CLEOPATRA: WHAT?! Ohhh... he's going to wish he were dead!!!

MESSENGER: Okayyyy, on that note, I'm outta here! *(exits frantically)*

CLEOPATRA: No wait! *(MESSENGER returns, scared)*

MESSENGER: Y-Y-Yes.

CLEOPATRA: Go back and spy on her. Tell me what she looks like, her age, hair color, the brands she wears. You know, the important things.

MESSENGER: That sounds very juvenile, almost high school.

CLEOPATRA: JUST DO IT!

MESSENGER: Yes, my queen!

(ALL exit)

ACT 2 SCENE 4

Italy

(POMPEY and his men enter from one side; ANTONY, CAESAR, LEPIDUS, and their men enter from other)

POMPEY: Are you ready to go to battle?

CAESAR: Are you ready to perish here?

LEPIDUS: Yeah, do the math. Three of us. One of you.

ANTONY: But we will make you a deal. You have a choice: die or...

LEPIDUS: OR... we give you Sicily and you must rid all the sea of pirates.

CAESAR: That's our offer. Death or your own private island!

(pause; EVERYONE hums Jeopardy theme)

POMPEY: I'll take the island! *(they all cheer)* Now, aboard my galley I invite you and we'll feast!

(ALL exit cheering)

ACT 3 SCENE 1

Caesar's house

(enter CAESAR, ANTONY, OCTAVIA, AGRIPPA, ENOBARBUS, and LEPIDUS)

LEPIDUS: *(stumbling)* THAT was an AWESOME party!!!

AGRIPPA: *(laughing)* Look at him!

ENOBARBUS: The fool is troubled with the green sickness, yet still wants to party!

LEPIDUS: Who you calling fool?! And... yeah! Woohoo!!!

(OCTAVIA and CAESAR hug)

OCTAVIA: My noble brother!

CAESAR: Farewell, my dearest Octavia. Antony, take good care of her, or you and I will... well, you know.

ANTONY: You insult me.

(LEPIDUS burps, interrupting their conversation)

LEPIDUS: Sorry! Please continue...

CAESAR: I was just saying...

ANTONY: I know what you were saying. Let's go, Octavia.

(ANTONY and OCTAVIA exit)

CAESAR: Farewell!

LEPIDUS: Well, that wasn't awkward or anything. *(pause)* Now let's get back to partying!!! Woohoo!!!

(ALL exit)

ACT 3 SCENE 2

Cleopatra's palace

(enter CLEOPATRA, IRAS, and CHARMIAN; MESSENGER from other side)

CHARMIAN: You're back already?

MESSENGER: It's a short play.

CLEOPATRA: Soooo... tell me, what's she like?

MESSENGER: Well, my queen, she's dull of tongue and dwarfish.

CLEOPATRA: You mean she's short, smelly, and rather plain looking! Yes!

IRAS: Excellent! Antony will be back in no time.

CLEOPATRA: Yay!

(ALL exit)

ACT 3 SCENE 3

Antony's house

(enter ANTONY and OCTAVIA)

ANTONY: Your brother's a piece of work!

OCTAVIA: What did he do now?

ANTONY: New wars 'gainst Pompey, and spoke scantly of me. ME! *(strikes a pose)* The Great Antony!

OCTAVIA: What do you want me to do about it?

ANTONY: Go back and spy on your brother for me.

OCTAVIA: So, I have to choose between you or my brother?

ANTONY: Choose wisely, Octavia. *(ANTONY exits)*

OCTAVIA: *(mocking)* Choose wisely. *(aside)* My brother, or my boyfriend? Oy!

(OCTAVIA exits)

ACT 3 SCENE 4

(enter ENOBARBUS and EROS)

EROS: Rumor Mill!

ENOBARBUS: What man?!

EROS: Caesar murder'd Pompey.

ENOBARBUS: What?! By himself?

EROS: Nope. He used Lepidus's army, and THEN put Lepidus in jail!

ENOBARBUS: WHAT?! Seriously? A total coup!!!

EROS: Yeah! Now Antony is headed for Italy and Caesar! Revenge!

ENOBARBUS: Nice exposition. This is going to be good!

(POMPEY enters)

POMPEY: Wait a minute... did I just hear you say that I'm dead?

ENOBARBUS: That be true, sir!

POMPEY: Darn! Well, that stinks! *(dies melodramatically)*

EROS: Such overactors...

ENOBARBUS: Right?

(ALL exit)

<h1 style="text-align:center">ACT 3 SCENE 5</h1>

Caesar's house

(enter CAESAR, AGRIPPA, and MAECENAS)

AGRIPPA: So, Caesar, how's it going?!

CAESAR: Horrible! Antony is back with Cleopatra sitting in chairs of gold.

MAECENAS: That bad, huh?

CAESAR: Worse! Now she's absolute queen of Syria, Cyprus, and Lydia!

AGRIPPA: Boy, can't get more troubling than that.

CAESAR: One would think, but now Antony wants some of the lands I conquered from Pompey!!!

MAECENAS: How rude!

CAESAR: Right!!!

AGRIPPA: Oh look, your sister!

(OCTAVIA enters)

CAESAR: Octavia! *(they hug)* Where's your fanfare? Your trumpeters?!

OCTAVIA: Oh, I don't have any.

CAESAR: What?! Antony's girlfriend, MY SISTER, should have an army for an usher!

OCTAVIA: Well, he sent me to make peace with you.

CAESAR: Oh, my most wronged sister, he's back together with Cleopatra.

OCTAVIA: What?! Noooooo!!! Boo hoo!!! Waaaaah!!!!

CAESAR: Come on, let's go hatch an evil revenge plan!

(ALL exit laughing evilly)

ACT 3 SCENE 6

Antony's camp, Greece

(enter ENOBARBUS and CLEOPATRA)

ENOBARBUS: Why, why, why join Antony in battle? You will be a distraction to him.

CLEOPATRA: Distraction?! *(tosses hair)* I fail to see how I could POSSIBLY be a distraction.

ENOBARBUS: Yeah... you're right. Never mind.

(enter ANTONY and CANIDIUS)

ANTONY: General Canidius, prepare our ships for battle against Caesar.

CLEOPATRA: I have sixty sails at your disposal as well.

CANIDIUS: Our navy will be ready sir, but...

ANTONY: Yes?

CANIDIUS: But, on land, Caesar's army is too strong, he will prevail.

ANTONY: Nonsense!

CLEOPATRA: General, celerity is never more admired than by the negligent.

ANTONY: A good rebuke.

CANIDIUS: Celery? Now is NOT the time to discuss vegetables!

ANTONY: CEL-ER-ITY not Celery!

CANIDIUS: Oh. Where do you get these fancy words?

CLEOPATRA: Shakespeare. It means swiftness. I read books too, you know. I'm not JUST a pretty girl.

CANIDIUS: Okaaay. *(aside)* Still doesn't make sense. On with the battle! *(ALL exit)*

ACT 3 SCENE 7

(stage is split, on one side CAESAR, AGRIPPA, and his SOLDIERS; the other ANTONY, CLEOPATRA, CANIDIUS, ENOBARBUS, and their men)

CAESAR: *(to his men)* Strike not by land, till we have done at sea!

SOLDIERS: Yes, sir!

ANTONY: Set our squadrons and proceed accordingly.

CANIDIUS: Yes, sir!

ANTONY: Enobarbus, stand here, look important, and tell the audience what is happening.

ENOBARBUS: Yes, sir!

(center stage a sea battle of ships ensues (toy boats or cardboard cut-outs) between CAESAR, CANIDIUS, ANTONY, and CLEOPATRA all saying "pew-pew!"; ENOBARBUS does play-by-play like sports announcer)

ENOBARBUS: Welcome to the great Battle of Actium! It looks as if Antony and Cleopatra are beating down Caesar and winning the battle!

(CLEOPATRA suddenly turns and leaves the stage)

ENOBARBUS: Oh no! Cleopatra hoists sails and flies!

ANTONY: Hey! Where are you going?!

CLEOPATRA: I don't know! But I'm out of here!

ANTONY: Well then... I guess I'll... I'll leave too!

CANIDIUS: Wait! Where are you going?! Cowards!

(ANTONY follows CLEOPATRA offstage)

ENOBARBUS: Alack, Alack! My eyes did sicken at the sight! Antony and Cleopatra fled, so... I guess Caesar wins!

CAESAR: Yay!!! Boy, that was lucky!

CANIDIUS: What just happened?!

CAESAR: You lost.

CANIDIUS: That's it! Caesar, I render my legions!

CAESAR: Great! Let's go celebrate!

(CANIDIUS, CAESAR, and his men exit cheering; ANTONY reenters)

ANTONY: I'm such a fool!

ENOBARBUS: Yep.

(ENOBARBUS exits; CLEOPATRA enters)

ANTONY: Cleo, how could you make me look like such a fool?

CLEOPATRA: O my lord, forgive my fearful sails! I little thought you would have follow'd.

ANTONY: Of course, I followed! You are my love. My heart was to thy rudder tied by the strings.

CLEOPATRA: Cute. Corny... but cute. I'm so sorry I caused you all this trouble. Forgive me? *(smiles beautifully)*

ANTONY: Of course, I could never be mad at you for long!

CLEOPATRA: Oh goody!

ANTONY: Now, I, The Great Antony, *(poses yet again!)* have to send humble treaties to Caesar.

CLEOPATRA: Again, so sorry! *(ALL exit)*

ACT 3 SCENE 8

(enter CAESAR, THIDIAS, and DOLABELLA)

DOLABELLA: That was a great battle! We were awesome!

THIDIAS: Yes, we were! *(all high five; enter MESSENGER)*

MESSENGER: Sir, I have a message from Antony.

CAESAR: Approach, and speak.

MESSENGER: Sir, it says that Antony begs you to let him live in Egypt, and if not, maybe a little cabin in Athens?

CAESAR: Is that all?

MESSENGER: Uhhh...no sir. Also, can you give Egypt to Cleopatra's heirs?

CAESAR: What! NOOOOO!!! I have no ears to his request.

MESSENGER: What then, sir?

CAESAR: Hmmm... Cleopatra can live as long as she either exiles or executes Antony. Easy-peasy!

MESSENGER: Very well, sir. *(exits)*

CAESAR: Thidias, lure Cleopatra into accepting my deal. Time to make Antony squirm.

THIDIAS: Caesar, I shall!

(ALL exit laughing evilly)

ACT 3 SCENE 9

Cleopatra's palace

(enter CLEOPATRA and ENOBARBUS)

CLEOPATRA: I feel guilty about Antony!

ENOBARBUS: You should.

CLEOPATRA: Huh? You're supposed to make me feel better!

ENOBARBUS: Oh, sorry. *(unconvincingly)* It's not your fault?

CLEOPATRA: *(rolls eyes)* Oh wow. Thanks.

(enter ANTONY)

ANTONY: I'm home!

(enter MESSENGER)

MESSENGER: Caesar says, "Ahhh... no."

ANTONY: Fine! Tell him I challenge him sword against sword for all the marbles!

MESSENGER: Sure thing! *(exits)*

ANTONY: I need to practice my sweet sword skills, I was once a great sworder! *(poses)* I shall be again! *(exits)*

(THIDIAS enters secretly)

THIDIAS: Psst! Psst!

CLEOPATRA: What do you want?

(ANTONY is peeking around and listening to their conversation)

THIDIAS: Caesar asks you to turn over Antony and he will grant you Egypt.

CLEOPATRA: Really? You think you can manipulate me?

THIDIAS: Yeah.

CLEOPATRA: You're right. I never really liked Antony, anyway.

(ANTONY shows shocked face)

THIDIAS: Great!

CLEOPATRA: Tell Caesar he is a god!

(ANTONY enters with SOLDIERS)

ANTONY: By Jove that thunders! *(ANTONY beats up THIDIAS)* Take him to the dungeon!

SOLDIER 1: We have a dungeon?

SOLDIER 2: *(shrugs)* Don't know. But don't ask. Antony is NOT in the mood!

SOLDIER 1: Ok. Let's just take him backstage.

SOLDIER 2: Good idea!

(SOLDIERS take THIDIAS away)

ANTONY: *(screaming)* I can't believe you were going to betray me!

CLEOPATRA: Who? Me?! Couldn't be! I would NEVER betray YOU!!!

ANTONY: *(suddenly calm)* Oh. Ok, then. I am satisfied.

CLEOPATRA: *(aside)* Whew!

ANTONY: You know... Our navy fleet is threatening most sea-like, and our force by land hath nobly held. I will oppose his fate!

CLEOPATRA: That's my brave lord!

(ANTONY and CLEOPATRA exit)

ENOBARBUS: Hmmm... note to self: seems like Antony is going a bit crazy. *(to audience)* Later!

(ALL exit)

ACT 4 SCENE 1

Caesar's camp, Egypt

(enter CAESAR and MAECENAS; enter MESSENGER from opposite)

MESSENGER: Caesar, Antony challenges you to personal combat.

(pause; CAESAR and MAECENAS laugh hysterically)

MAECENAS: You're funny!!!

CAESAR: Antony is weak and pathetic. Tell the old ruffian, NO!

(CAESAR and MAECENAS exit; ANTONY, EROS, ENOBARBUS, and SOLDIERS enter opposite)

ANTONY: Well?

MESSENGER: Ummm, sir... they laughed in your face.

ANTONY: WHAT?!

MESSENGER: Sir, Caesar said, 'I have many other ways to die. Laugh at his challenge.' *(laughs until ANTONY pulls sword; MESSENGER runs offstage)*

ANTONY: Then by sea and land I'll fight!

SOLDIER 2: Are you sure you want to do that, sir?

ANTONY: Yes! I will live or die by honour!

SOLDIER 1: But, sir...

ANTONY: Stop! It's all about my ego! Haply you shall not see me more, or if, a mangled shadow. I deserve my fate.

SOLDIER 2: Wow. How depressing.

ENOBARBUS: Yeah, way to motivate. Woohoo...

ANTONY: Oh, sorry. Well... I'm sure we will all live? *(very unsure)*

ALL: *(very apathetic)* Yay!

(enter CLEOPATRA)

CLEOPATRA: My dearest, I'll help too.

ANTONY: I think you've helped enough. I will be back soon, my love.

EROS: Sir, a thousand soldiers at the port expect you. Well, except Enobarbus.

ANTONY: What? He is standing right here.

ENOBARBUS: Ahhh, yeah... about that... I'm not going to be there.

ANTONY: Why not?

ENOBARBUS: Well, I think you've gone nuts and I am not supporting you anymore. Love you like a brother, but like a brother in a nuthouse. Sorry, bro!

ANTONY: Makes sense, but... that stinks. Gentle adieus, Enobarbus. Take all thy treasure with, as a thank you. Eros, Are you ready?

EROS: Yes, sir.

ANTONY: Great, then lead the way.

EROS: Yes, sir! You heard him, men. Charge!!!

(ALL exit, with ANTONY following; ENOBARBUS remains)

ENOBARBUS: *(to audience)* Well, great, now I feel guilty. So guilty, I will go seek some ditch wherein to die. Let's see... not that ditch... no, not that one... there! That's a good ditch! Bye-bye.

(ENOBARBUS falls over dead)

ACT 4 SCENE 2

Cleopatra's palace

(ANTONY and SCARUS enter; CLEOPATRA enters opposite)

SCARUS: Antony, we were glorious in battle today!

ANTONY: Yes, we were, Scarus! Tomorrow, Caesar will fall!

(they do elaborate handshake)

CLEOPATRA: Com'st thou smiling from the war?

SCARUS: Yes! Antony was amazing! He fought as though he did not like mankind!

ANTONY: But I love YOUR kind, Cleo.

CLEOPATRA: Ahhh, you're so cute, Tony!

ANTONY: Yes. Yes, I am. *(poses – kissing biceps)* Let's go celebrate!

(ALL exit)

ACT 4 SCENE 3

Field of battle between camps

(enter ANTONY and SCARUS)

ANTONY: Caesar will attack us today by sea, but Cleopatra's ships will help us.

SCARUS: Let's watch the battle from this hill.

ANTONY: Good idea.

SCARUS: Oh, would you look at that, Cleopatra just surrendered and joined Caesar.

ANTONY: All is lost! The foul Egyptian has betrayed me.

SCARUS: It looks that way, sir.

ANTONY: Hmmm... well, this certainly stinks!

SCARUS: Sooooo, what should we do?

ANTONY: Run, Scarus. RUN!!! Go now!

SCARUS: Aghhhh!!!

(SCARUS runs offstage)

ANTONY: Cleopatra is evil!!! I will be revenged upon my charm.

(CLEOPATRA enters)

ANTONY: Ah, thou spell! Avaunt!

CLEOPATRA: What?!

ANTONY: GET OUT OF HERE!!!

(ANTONY chases CLEOPATRA offstage, both are crazy screaming)

ACT 4 SCENE 4

Cleopatra's palace

(enter CLEOPATRA, IRAS, and CHARMIAN from opposite)

CLEOPATRA: Help me, my women! Oh, he's mad! Crazy, I tell you!

CHARMIAN: Who?

CLEOPATRA: WHO?! Antony, that's who!

IRAS: Why?

CLEOPATRA: I dunno, something about betraying him. I was too busy screaming and running to hear anything.

IRAS: Well, did you betray him?

CLEOPATRA: Who, me? Yeah.

CHARMIAN: I have an idea, why don't you send word that you killed yourself!

CLEOPATRA: Ohhhh, very Romeo and Juliet!

CHARMIAN: Who?

CLEOPATRA: Nevermind, that's still a few hundred years away.

CHARMIAN: Oh.

CLEOPATRA: But, great idea, go tell him I have slain myself!

(ALL exit)

(enter ANTONY and EROS)

ANTONY: Give me my sword, Eros. It is time that I vanquish Cleopatra!

(enter MESSENGER; ANTONY pulls sword on him)

ANTONY: What do you want?

MESSENGER: Woah! Ever heard of the term 'don't kill the messenger'?

ANTONY: Fine! What's your message?

MESSENGER: To tell you Cleopatra killed herself.

ANTONY: WHAT?! NOOOOOOOO!!!!

MESSENGER: Yes. Her last words were, "Antony! Most noble Antony!"

ANTONY: NOOOOOOOO!!!!

MESSENGER: Again, yes. Goodbye. *(exits)*

ANTONY: Eros, I am disgrace and horror. Thou wouldst kill me: do't. *(hands sword to EROS, who drops it)*

EROS: Ewwww, no!

ANTONY: What?! Draw and come.

EROS: Agh! Fine. My sword is drawn. Farewell.

ANTONY: Yes. Farewell.

EROS: Shall I strike now?

ANTONY: Yes, now!

(EROS stabs himself)

EROS: Ok, bye! *(dies)*

ANTONY: What?! O valiant Eros. Thou teaches me. *(stabs self)* How! Not dead? Not dead?!

(DIOMEDES enters)

DIOMEDES: Antony?

ANTONY: Yeah? *(he falls to knee in pain)*

DIOMEDES: Ahh... Cleopatra sent you word she was dead, but... she's not.

ANTONY: What?!

DIOMEDES: Surprise!

ANTONY: *(drops to both knees)* Bear me where Cleopatra bides. I am dying, Egypt, dying.

DIOMEDES: Ok, but this is a new toga, don't get it all bloody.

(DIOMEDES helps ANTONY offstage)

ACT 4 SCENE 6

Cleopatra's palace

(enter CLEOPATRA, CHARMIAN, and IRAS; enter DIOMEDES and ANTONY opposite)

DIOMEDES: I'm baaack, and I brought someone!

CHARMIAN: Who?

DIOMEDES: Antony!!!

CLEOPATRA: Oh, yay!!!

DIOMEDES: But, he's going to die.

CLEOPATRA: Oh, noooo!

ANTONY: I love you!

CLEOPATRA: I love you!

ANTONY: I love you more!

CLEOPATRA: No! I love you more!

ANTONY: NO! I love... Achhhh... *(poses one last time, then falls over dead)*

IRAS: Hmmm, I think he loved you.

CLEOPATRA: The crown o'th' Earth doth melt. Oh, this is my fault! *(weeping)* What am I to do?

DIOMEDES: Well, if Caesar captures you, he'll parade your body around the streets for all to see.

CHARMIAN: Ahhh, not helping.

DIOMEDES: Oops! Sorry!

CLEOPATRA: I must be with my Antony again. *(ugly cries as ALL exit)*

ACT 5 SCENE 1

Caesar's camp

(enter CAESAR and AGRIPPA; MESSENGER from opposite carrying sword)

CAESAR: What are you doing with a sword?

MESSENGER: Antony is dead. This is his sword.

CAESAR: What? How did that happen?

MESSENGER: Well, you see, Cleopatra…

CAESAR: Stop, you've said enough! Who killed him?

MESSENGER: Not by a hired knife, but that self hand who did all the great deeds that Antony is known for!

CAESAR: What?

MESSENGER: He killed himself.

CAESAR: Oh, I see what you did there.

MESSENGER: Clever, huh?

CAESAR: Very. We must mourn such an extraordinary man. The breaking of so great a thing should make a greater crack.

AGRIPPA: Ummm, weren't we just trying to kill him a few scenes ago?

CAESAR: Yeah, but I'm past that. It's now ok to weep for our loss.

AGRIPPA: Okey-dokey, boss!

MESSENGER: Oh, and the queen desires instructions of your intentions.

CAESAR: Bid her have good heart. I plan her no harm.

MESSENGER: Yes, sir. *(exits)*

CAESAR: Actually, I'll parade her through Rome eternal in our triumph! Bwahahaha!!!

AGRIPPA: Wow. You are really evil. Nice!

CAESAR: Thank you, it's one of my better qualities. Go with your speediest to make sure she doesn't spoil my plan!

AGRIPPA: Caesar, I shall!

(ALL exit)

ACT 5 SCENE 2

Alexandria

(enter CLEOPATRA, IRAS, and CHARMIAN)

CLEOPATRA: Ladies, I do not trust Caesar.

CHARMIAN: No, you shouldn't. It is best you take matters into your own hands.

(enter DOLABELLA grabs CLEOPATRA)

DOLABELLA: I'll take the queen to my guard until Caesar arrives.

IRAS: What are Caesar's plans?

DOLABELLA: Oh, nothing.

CHARMIAN: Something I'm sure. What, Dolabella?

IRAS: What?!

DOLABELLA: Nothing! Nothing!

IRAS & CHARMIAN: WHAT!?!?!

DOLABELLA: Okay, okay. He'll lead her in triumph through Rome... FOREVER.

IRAS: Wow.

CHARMIAN: That stinks.

(DOLABELLA goes to side)

CLEOPATRA: Sure does. Not going to let that happen. But, hark thee, Charmian and Iras.

CHARMIAN & IRAS: Yes?

CLEOPATRA: Get the snakes.

IRAS: The asps?! Oh, the good gods! But they'll kill you!

CLEOPATRA: Exactly! Go put it to the haste.

(CHARMIAN exits and returns with snakes)

CHARMIAN: Okay, one for each of us!

DOLABELLA: What are you ladies doing over there?

CHARMIAN, IRAS, & CLEOPATRA: Nothing!

DOLABELLA: Oh good. For a second, I thought you were up to something.

CLEOPATRA: NOW!

(all three are bitten and die most melodramatic deaths)

CLEOPATRA: Now no more the juice of Egypt's grape shall moist these lips. *(dies)*

(enter CAESAR and AGRIPPA)

CAESAR: What's this?!

AGRIPPA: It looks as if they are dead.

CAESAR: No kidding. Bummer, she spoiled all my fun!

AGRIPPA: What shall we do?

CAESAR: She shall be buried by her Antony. As for us...

AGRIPPA: Yes...

CAESAR: We get to rule the world!

(maniacal laugh as ALL exit)

THE END

Special Thanks

Thank you's... Angi and Elijah, always great humor from those two! Big thanks to Rosemary (or should I say, DOCTOR Rosemary about now?!). Jean, thank you for your feedback and for bringing melodramatic Shakespeare to the kids for the past decade! Catherine, thank you so much for all your wonderful and creative suggestions!

Huge thanks to Mrs. Miller's Fourth-grade class from Horn Elementary. Those are some funny kids! Great feedback!!!

Dave, as always, you speak the truth and say what I don't necessarily want to hear but needs to be heard. Thank you for your frankness!

Other beta reader thanks: Sandra, Meredith, David, Isidro, Laura, Khara (always pushing me to be better with my grammar!)

And finally, a huge thanks to the biggest poser, Roy R. Thanks for being creative and funny! (author strikes Alexander-type pose but inadvertantly pokes self in eye while holding a pencil he doesn't even use, but wanting to look author-like. He goes down like a crumpling mass of mashed potatoes and manages to squeak out, "thanks!")

-Brendan

ABOUT THE AUTHOR

BRENDAN P. KELSO came to writing modified Shakespeare scripts when he was taking time off from work to be at home with his newly born son. "It just grew from there". Within months, he was being asked to offer classes in various locations and acting organizations along the Central Coast of California. Originally employed as an engineer, Brendan never thought about writing. However, his unique personality, humor, and love for engaging the kids with The Bard has led him to leave the engineering world and pursue writing as a new adventure in life! He has always believed, "the best way to learn is to have fun!" Brendan makes his home on the Central Coast of California and loves to spend time with his wife and kids.

CAST AUTOGRAPHS